Anti-Feminism - Why we should all be Equalists

Mens Rights, Feminazis, Equalism and Feminists

By Gary Snow

I0412129

GARY SNOW

CONTENTS

1. INTRODUCTION

I'm not saying all feminists are bad by a long shot. But it makes me so angry that there is a fresh batch of so called feminists that are giving a bad name to the first wave feminists that fought for their rights through women's suffrage by using this name as a mask for their avocation of female supremacy.

First wave feminists came about in the early 20th century and I think they did fantastic work. 2nd wave feminists came about in the 60's and they focused on issues that also had relevance. 3rd wave Feminism that we have these days however is not real feminism at all. 3rd wave feminism is oppressive, totalitarian and exhibits many signs of fascism.

There are two main groups of modern 3rd wave feminists. You have the Pseudo Feminists, and the Radical Feminists.

Pseudo feminists are usually around 15-25 and generally haven't truly looked into 3rd wave feminism properly, they just associate feminism with women's rights because of the propaganda they see online and the history behind the name "Feminism". So they don't really know what the movement they are claiming to be a part of truly stands for.

Radical 3rd wave feminists are sexist, female supremacists. They are totalitarians who twist and manipulate statistics to create propaganda to attract impressionable girls and women to their cause. They are also very quick to rally their naive Pseudo Feminist supporters into online hate campaigns to silence and persecute people for having any difference of opinion to them.

Modern 3rd wave feminism is such a dangerous tool because by using the name "Feminists", they have attached the good deeds of other women to their cause making most people blind to the evil that lies beneath. What used to be a worthy cause started by brave women who stood up for themselves in the face of direct oppression for their right to vote and own property, is now the tool of a group of professionally offended man haters.

The original first wave feminists obviously passed away long ago, and therefore cannot disassociate themselves from 3rd wave feminism. It's a bit like starting a war in the name of Jesus even though he preached peace, he's not around to say that he doesn't support the war but he is associated with starting it anyway. It's all propaganda.

Let me make one thing completely clear before I get any further. I don't hate or even dislike women, at all. If I ever have a daughter one day I want her to be able to go through life without the fear of men acting inappropriately towards her. But, I also don't want her head filled with ridiculous, false feminist propaganda about all men being some sort of oppressors.

GARY SNOW

2. THE PROBLEM WITH FEMINISM

The main problem with 3rd wave feminism is that it's not synonymous with women's rights. There are many underlying values that align far better with female supremacy. Let me say that again. Modern Feminism...is not synonymous with women's rights.

This year, while news reports of a pregnant women being stoned to death in Pakistan for marrying a man that wasn't chosen for her were emerging, feminists were in an online frenzy. Not about this though, they were far more concerned with their ability to post photos of their nipples without them getting removed by Instagram. I will let you decide which one of these issues is more important to women's rights.

Also earlier this year, a group of feminists decided to start the twitter hashtag of #KillAllMen. Around this time Isis was asking twitter how they should execute a Jordanian pilot they had captured, but the feminists were too busy tweeting #KillAllMen to notice this of course.

See a trend here? Modern day feminism has lost all of its previous direction, focusing on trivial and pointless first world issues while ignoring the problems that actually matter.

One of the core values of feminism and a principle that feminism is built on is equality. Every feminist knows that Feminists want equality right? But how can you fight for gender equality when you're only tackling the issues of one gender? It's a ridiculous concept to say the very least. Any movement that claims to advocate equality and then chooses a gender specific name obviously has something wrong with it.

Now in response to this, Feminists will probably say "But the inequality that exists between the sexes favors men and subjugates women." Really? Maybe once it did back when Feminism was founded and it was still relevant. But that's simply not true anymore as I will go on to prove time and time again in this book. Feminists believe this because they haven't looked at the facts and instead blindly believe the one sided propaganda that is being fed to them by Radical Feminists.

A major fact that feminism completely ignores is that men are actually, in many ways, far worse off than women in modern society. Examples of men being at a disadvantage to women include child custardy and child support payments. Women are also given, on average, 40% less time in prison then men for committing the exact same crimes. Still to this day, women are not legally obliged to carry out national service in the armed forces if conscription was to occur. If a world war were to break out, men have to fight and die just because their government told them to, women don't. Imagine if we flied this around and actually gave modern Feminists something real to complain about. All hell would break loose.

If women in fact do want equality between the sexes and don't just care about themselves, then surely they would identify far more with being an equalist. The problem is that most modern feminists don't want this, they want everything their way.

As I said, 3rd wave radical Feminists are totalitarians who will silence anyone who disagrees with them by ganging up and bullying them. A great example of this is when Kaley Cuoco said, "I like the idea of women taking care of their men" and feminists started an online hate campaign in response.

They can't stand it when other people, male or female, say anything they don't agree with. It is Kaley's right as a human being to say what she wants and to look after anyone she wants, but they stood against these basic human rights because it didn't fit in line with their views.

While accepting the women of the year award Katy Perry said "I am not a feminist, but I do believe in the strength of women." Well that's fair enough isn't it. She just isn't a part of the 3rd wave modern feminism movement. Nothing wrong with that. Well according to feminists, who immediately began tearing her apart via social media, she's not allowed to not be a feminist.

She didn't even disagree with them, she just stated that she wasn't one of them. That was enough however and the feminist backlash that ensued is further proof that modern feminists are totalitarians who will not accept anything other than absolute dominance.

They don't want to kill the king to abolish the monarchy, they want to kill the king so that they can become the queen.

The Nazis only had the support of 10% of the German population, but they remained in power by silencing anyone who opposed them. Now what happens when anyone opposes modern feminist ideology? They instantly try to silence them. The sad thing is, the people on the receiving end of these campaigns almost always end up giving in and apologising. In other words, they are silenced.

So by doing this, they can remain unchallenged by removing peoples freedom of speech, just as the Nazis did. I'm not saying feminists are as bad as the Nazis obviously, but fascist ethics and totalitarianism seem to be common themes in the way modern feminists are acting towards any opposing opinions.

What are they so scared of? In my experience, if an idea doesn't stand up under scrutiny then it's because it's not a very good idea.

3. DOMESTIC VIOLENCE

Domestic violence towards women is a major talking point in feminism. I have seen my male best friends face with his blood red eye, a split lip and a chipped off tooth from the time his girlfriend repeatedly beat him and kicked him in the face while he was laying on the floor. I also saw him go back to her time and time again only for the same emotional and physical abuse to continue. But he's a man so feminism ignores him because they don't deem this to be as important as domestic violence the issues facing women.

These days, reported cases of domestic violence against men is almost as common as domestic violence against women. Men are far less likely to report it due to embarrassment so we can safely assume the levels are pretty equal.

But feminists only fight to stop domestic violence against women. No one seems to care about domestic violence against men. The police don't take it anywhere near as seriously, the courts don't, the media doesn't and people in general don't. In this respect men are actually worse off than women if anything.

There is a TV show called "The Talk" that you may have heard of, where a group of five women discuss things. On one particular episode of this show the 5 women, including Sharon Osborne, were talking about a woman who cut her husband's penis off in his sleep because he asked her for a divorce. She actually took a knife, and cut off his penis and then threw it down the garbage disposal. This is a sick woman who has mutilated another human being in an act of extreme domestic violence.

But for some reason these 5 women, and the whole studio audience of women, found this story incredibly funny. They were laughing and smirking as the story was being read out. Sharon then went on to say "I do think it's quite fabulous" and "It's hysterical." And even "I would have just thrown it in the dogs bowl." Yes she is saying that if she were to cut off a man's penis with a knife, she would have then fed it to a dog. At which point the audience gave out a tremendous roar of laughter.

Then one of the other women brought up the Lorena Bobbitt case where, she too cut off her husband's penis with a knife. To which Sharon then stated "Love her. Love her. I light candles by her picture."

Thankfully one of these women did decide to be a, "buzzkill" as she called herself. She mentioned the fact that if a man cut a woman's breasts off they wouldn't be laughing, which is exactly what I was thinking too. But Sharon decides to jump back in with "It's different though." Now that's the first thing she has said that was actually right, it is different. But only in the way that it's more like removing a woman's vagina and clitoris. But still they laughed on.

Does this sound hard to believe to you? It should do. If you don't believe my very accurate description of this, look it up on YouTube.

Now they did issue an apology for doing this but the underlying fact that these women and the entire studio audience, thought it was perfectly acceptable to sit there laughing ravenously about a men being permanently mutilated by a woman in an extreme case of domestic violence.

This just shows how much of a huge gap there is between domestic violence against men and domestic violence against women. Men have things way worse. So if someone is a feminist due to domestic violence, unless they believe that the behavior I have described in this chapter is acceptable, then they should in fact be an equalist fighting for an end to domestic violence for both men and women.

4. THE PATRIARCHY

Feminists constantly reference the patriarchy as the cause for all of women's woes throughout history. The main they thing are getting wrong in this respect is that they have the causality completely backwards.

The Patriarchy is the system that puts men as the leaders, from men being in power in the government to men being the head of the household. Feminists believe that patriarchy is the very reason gender roles exist in modern society and the reason those roles are defined how they are.

But the patriarchy is not the cause of gender roles at all. The patriarchy is the direct result of gender roles that have been defined since before we were even civilized human beings. Evidence of gender roles can be seen throughout the animal kingdom in the most basic, primal sense and we as a species we are no different.

So the patriarchy that feminists blame almost everything on is actually caused by gender roles and the way we view men and women differently because of our basic genetic differences and abilities. The patriarchy was not created to oppress women like feminists seem to think, it is simply the product of our progression into modern civilization and the incorporation of those already existing gender roles.

True, the patriarchy and the subjugation of women is still common place in various countries around the world. But all the first world man haters identifying themselves as feminists while sitting behind their keyboards on their laptop or smartphone, that they bought for themselves, after a day at work tweeting to the world about the patriarchy, don't even realize that the patriarchy doesn't exist anymore in western society. What we do have are remnants of gender roles from our evolution, not male oppression.

This "modern day patriarchy" feminists constantly reference is fundamentally not patriarchy at all. If it was and men wanted solely to run the world, why would we create a system that disadvantages us at all? Patriarchy by definition, solely benefits men. It's a system that is completely dominated by men, so if patriarchy is real today, why would we have any part of that system that didn't benefit us? We wouldn't! Therefore patriarchy and the very thing that feminists began to rebel against all those years ago, doesn't even exist anymore. What does exist is gender related issues for both men AND women.

Modern feminism is telling women to think that gender roles are wrong and not to conform to them. Yes, feminists are telling other women how to behave. What if a woman wants to stay at home and not go out to work every day? What if she actually enjoys cooking and looking after her children? She shouldn't be made to believe she is a lesser person for doing so. Men wouldn't tell her she's less of a woman for doing this, feminists would.

Besides this, the way that women look after the children and men go out and bring home the bacon is something that has been a part of human culture since before we even were humans and look how far we have come. But now due to the new breed of feminists this idea is being distorted in women's heads and turned into something evil. It's not evil it's just basic human nature that women should not be made to feel bad about.

Obviously if a woman want's to work and not stay at home to look after her children, she has every right to do so due to the fact there is no patriarchy anymore. Get a nanny. But to tell women that staying at home and looking after your children is outdated and a part of a suppressive patriarchal system is wrong. Don't poison them against the idea and make them feel oppressed for doing something they want to do.

5. THEY WANT IT ALL

Now I know a fair few women that call themselves feminists, and even women that aren't feminists, who want equal rights and don't like gender roles that mean they have to stay at home and cook or look after the kids. Yet they still want to keep the gender roles that mean men have to buy them constant gifts and take them out for meals. Shocking isn't it.

They can't have both without admitting their superiority complex. They need to either split the bills when they're on dates and hold doors open for men or accept gender roles and admit that they don't actually want equal rights, they want superiority. Acting in way is practically narcissistic. But it's ok because there is words they use to cover it up like chivalry and gentleman.

The thing you need to remember when talking about chivalry and gentlemen is that these ideas were put in place for balance. A balance that is now swinging firmly in the favor of women. In a patriarchal system where men made all the decisions, men got more respect and controlled all of the money. In return men spent this money on women and were far kinder to women in general by speaking to them politely, buying them gifts, taking them for meals and opening doors for them for example. This created both the notions of chivalry and being a gentleman.

But now that women can also earn money and demand respect, own land, vote and have all the other privileges that a man can have, why do women keep referencing these outdated notions of men being chivalrous gentlemen? Because it benefits them massively.

To put it another way, women seem to be hanging on to the romanticized notion of a knight in shining armor who will sweep them off their feet. Well they can't have a knight in shining armor come and save them if they're also a knight in shining armor capable of saving themselves now can they?

But that's what they want anyway, and this knight has to not only save this other knight that has the ability to save themselves, but also pay for this other knight and buy gifts for them. Is this sounding one sided yet? I think we're closing in quickly on the realization that 3rd wave Feminists genuinely do have a massive superiority complex.

Then these women who expect all of this, sit around after men leave them for obvious reasons wondering why they're single. They will complain about how there is no good guys that will pay for them to get a pedicure and eventually conclude that men are just selfish pigs that only want one thing.

The bottom line is these women shouldn't complain that they deserve gifts purely for the fact that they have a pair of breasts and a vagina unless they want to be treated like a pair of breats and a vagina instead of an equal.

GARY SNOW

6. PSEUDO FEMINISTS

Unfortunately, it seems that the content of 3rd wave Feminist propaganda campaigns have completely manifested themselves in many a young and impressionable girls mind via the internet. Provoking them into a blind stance of pseudo feminist activism against first world problems.

For example this book is called "Anti-Feminism", that alone is going to be enough to make these brainwashed girls and women think this is a hateful book made by a man who wants to subjugate and control women. I'm not at all, I just don't agree with the modern feminist movement. But they are made to believe through propaganda, that anyone who doesn't like Feminism is some sort of monster.

Now I don't think men should be allowed to lay their hands on a woman in any way without consent, just as a woman shouldn't be able to touch a man without the same consent. However, a favorite topic of these pseudo feminists seems to be having men telling them they're good looking or slapping their butt and how this is worse than anything that could possibly ever happen to anyone. And they throw around terms like "rape culture" because they heard it in some biased feminist propaganda that is geared to make them hate men. It just so happens that these young girls get to also brag at the same time about how much they get hit on.

Bonus!

I see posts all the time talking about this kind of thing, teenage girls complaining about how a man looked their boobs instead of into their eyes and how this means we live in a "rape culture". Then you look at their profile pictures and practically all of them have their boobs hanging out while pulling a duck face. But no they don't like it when men look at them lustfully according to their posts.

Most of these social media posts are accompanied by the statement "This is why I'm a feminist." Which is completely ridiculous considering none of these girls do anything to contribute to the feminist movement other than complain via social media about how all men are pigs and write #feminism at the end.

Oh they might also like or share a post on Facebook to show that they don't agree with rape. This may come as a bit of a shock to them, but you don't need to be a feminist to know that rape is wrong or to share a Facebook post.

These are the sort of feminists that wear those annoying "This is what a feminist looks like" t-shirts that sell for £45 a pop, and are worn by people who will mostly never take any action other than wearing that t-shirt to make it look like they are making a difference to the world. Well did you know that those t-shirts were made by women that are paid 62p an hour and slept in a room with 15 other women in a sweat shop? Another win for feminism!

Imagine being one of those women who are truly subjugated and living in squalor. Making t-shirts for girls who claim to support feminism, yet they can justify spending £45 on one t-shirt, only to be lining the pockets of a people cashing in on gullible young pseudo feminists. The irony of that situation isn't even close to funny.

I actually saw one of these pseudo feminists saying that she was a feminist because having never experienced street harassment, she now felt unattractive. Yes, she was actually complaining that other women got more compliments than her in public.

This is typical of pseudo feminism, they will complain about anything and everything and validate it by attributing their views to feminism. By doing this they have the support of all the other pseudo feminists when anyone opposes their opinion even if it is wrong. These are Radical Feminists in the making.

GARY SNOW

7. MAGAZINES AND THE MEDIA

I do agree that a lot of magazines do over scrutinize women's figures and their clothes, especially those of celebrities and I don't think this is right. But let's face the facts. Judging other people, and everything else in this world, is part of human nature.

We judge women on their figure, we judge men on their physique, we judge children on their grades, we judge the homeless for being dirty and smelling bad and we judge pretty much everything else based on superficial information. You probably judged this book by its title and of course the cover before reading it.

It's true that men don't get scrutinized for what they wear as much as women in these magazines. Or if they get a bit fat no one cares as much as if it was a fat women. But who are those magazines aimed at? Who buys them and therefore supports their behavior? Women.

How many men's magazines do you think talk about how some z list celebrity from a reality TV show that we have never heard of lost 20lb in a month? None.

Besides all this, men are judged constantly too. I can tell you that I have been told multiple times by women that I should start working out and lifting weights because girls would find me more attractive if I did. How many times have I told a woman that she should get down the gym and lose some weight to make herself more attractive to men? Never! Because it's rude to do that, so why do women think its ok to say these things to me? Because society says it's ok. Just another example of how men are at a disadvantage to women in many respects.

So when you think about how women are so hard done by because they are put under pressure to look good, this pressure is caused by women. Men have it just as bad as women anyway, we just don't complain about it as much because most of us don't really care about our appearances as much as women seem to. You may think that sounds like a generalization but why do most women spend so long doing their nails, hair and putting makeup on in order to make their face look better? Because women are generally more vain than men. Sorry, but in general, that statement is true.

If I saw a man in a perfume advert with his shirt undone to show off his abs, I wouldn't think "Right it's the end of the world, male sexuality is being exploited to sell this companies product. I'm now going to join a movement founded on outdated issues in order to show my hatred of these marketing tactics." I would just think, yeah there's a good looking guy standing under a waterfall showing off his toned stomach in order to help this company get sales, and that's his choice. Big deal.

Sexuality is a thing, it just so happens that more people find slimmer girls more attractive than larger girls so those are the ones they use in advertising. Feminists seem to have a problem with this because they say that advertising is showing women they have to be stick thin to be desirable to men. This is a complete exaggeration as these stick thin models you're talking about are mainly catwalk models, most of the models and actresses on TV are a pretty healthy size. How many men do you think watch catwalks?

Also, these 3rd wave feminists complain about being noticed for their appearance when they meet someone and they say this is wrong. This is probably one of the most moronic statements I have ever heard. Of course you're going to be judged on your appearance, just like everyone else! What's feminism going to do to resolve this? Make all men wear blackout sunglasses until they have spoken to a woman for half an hour first? Blind auditions for job interviews?

Television shows and cartoons do reinforce gender roles. You just have to look at shows like The Simpsons, Family Guy, The Flintstones and a multitude of sitcoms. They all have the same theme. They show girls that women stay at home and the men go out and work. But I would say men have it worse here too. In these family scenarios the men are always idiots and the women are always the smart ones who wear the trousers and basically divert the men from their path of sure-fire self-destruction.

How many times on TV have you seen a woman talk about how women are smarter or better than men? It happens all the time, but god forbid a man says that men are superior to women. The backlash from that would be huge.

In music there are women like Beyoncé, who is a feminist, who actually writes lyrics like "Who runs the word? Girls." This sort of supremacy complex glorifying rubbish is being pumped out to girls who will grow up thinking they are perfectly entitled to believe they are superior to men.

Does feminism care about that? No, because they don't stand for equality, they only care about the issues that they deem harmful to women.

8. SEXISM IN THE WORKPLACE

If you have looked into feminism at all you undoubtedly would have heard the constantly repeated statistic that for every dollar a man makes a woman only makes 77 cents on average. This cornerstone fact that so many arguments for modern day feminism rely on is fantastically misleading and in fact, completely wrong.

It doesn't take into account the differences in occupations or even the hours worked per week. For a true statistical representation of average earnings to back up these feminist arguments that say women get paid less for the same amount of work, you obviously need to compare people in the same job working the same hours. Yet this 77% statistic completely ignores that simple fact.

Let's apply some real work logic to this fallacy shall we? If the wage gap was a real thing then I can tell you exactly what would happen. We would see a huge drop in employment for men as companies would realize they could get the same amount of work done for less money by simply employing more women. Has that happened? Of course not, because the wage gap doesn't exist.

I have also seen feminists complaining about how women make up a very small percentage of the building and engineering trades. Yes, because hardly any women actually want to do that for a job!

Is feminism going to round up women and force them into engineering and everything else to ensure a 50-50 split of men and women in each industry?

While we're at it, did you know that 100% of male strippers are men? What an outrage! We better round up the women and get them into some speedos and down to a hen party as soon as possible.

Another main talking point among feminists is that men see women in managerial positions as being moody and bossy with a bad attitude. There was even a huge campaign that you may have seen where celebrities banded together, including Beyoncé of course, to ban the word "Bossy". Yes, feminists actually want to ban a word because they don't like it. You can't just ban a word!

Men dislike male bosses and managers too you know and call them bossy. It's not a gender issue, it's an issue of being unhappy in your job and having to answer to another person whether they be male or female.

Oh and female comedians, well that's a hot topic for modern day feminism too apparently. I don't know if it has ever occurred to the women complaining about this particular topic that they might not actually be very funny. No it can't be that, it has to be that men don't laugh at their jokes because they are too busy wondering why she's on stage and not in the kitchen. What are these feminists hoping to achieve? To tell men they have to find non-funny comedians funny just because they are women?

9. RAPE AND SEXUAL ABUSE

A surprisingly high number of women do experience some sort of attempted rape or are actually raped in their lives. One of my best female friends is a victim of attempted rape. This is obviously sickening and is a big problem.

A very small percentage of accused rapists are actually convicted due to the fact that it usually comes down to one person's word against another.

But, if anything, Feminism is actually undermining real rape victims by classing any kind of sexual harassment as some kind of rape. They throw the word rape around way too much. Some Feminists class any sex where there wasn't some kind of verbal contract in place as rape. This sounds like I'm being over dramatic but it's true.

They have actually said that you need to actually verbally ask a woman if she wants to have sex before doing it otherwise it's rape. So even though the woman may have made it obvious she wants to have sex, you have to stop and ask them to confirm it.

So imagine a woman has invited a man into her home after a date, she then asks him into the bedroom and starts taking her clothes off. If a man then has sex with this woman, in the eyes of these feminists, this man is a rapist unless he say's something like

"Do you want to have sex?" Of course she does! It's ridiculous.

Now in my experience, if a woman doesn't want to kiss you or to have sex, they won't. Many of my female friends have told me stories about how a guy asked if he could kiss them and said that it was incredibly awkward.

Here are some real quotes from high profile feminists that further undermine the severity of rape which you can verify with a quick google search:

1.   "Marriage is an institution that is developed from rape as a practice."

2.   "All sex, even consensual sex between a married couple, is an act of violence perpetrated against a woman."

3.   "Heterosexual intercourse is the pure formalized expression of contempt for women's bodies."

4.   "Romance is rape embellished with meaningful looks."

5.   "Every woman's son is son is her potential betrayer and also the inevitable rapist or exploiter of another woman."

These quotes are effectively spitting in the face of real rape victims the world over. These statements all discredit feminism and add more weight to argument that feminism is mainly a group of female supremacist man haters who over react and complain about irrelevant issues that any sane person would find perfectly acceptable.

Modern 3rd wave feminism is not equipped to deal with problems like rape anyway. A group of people getting together and making a point can do a lot to alter systems and establishment but they can't change the minds of rapists. It's too simplistic to just think "Well I don't agree with rape so I'm going to say I'm a feminist."

Another main point that a lot of feminists seem to use is that society is trying to teach them how to not get raped or been seen as sexual by men who may want to behave inappropriately towards them. When in actual fact society should be telling men not to rape not showing women how to not get raped.

Well, news flash, we already do try to tell people not to rape! And we do it without the help of feminism. If society could stop rapists then it would have already. Rape isn't committed by people who don't know that rape is wrong, it's committed by people who don't care.

So the next best thing we can do is to advise women on how to avoid it and protect themselves if it does happen. I don't know how feminists could have a problem with this as it's the only thing that can be done to try and help the problem. But no, they are incredibly insulted by this sensible notion of self-defense and prefer to live in their dream world where all rapists will one day see the light and just stop raping. Or maybe they will #KillAllMen.

Here's one last thing for you to think about on this topic. If a man and a woman get blind drunk and have sex, she's considered a victim and he's considered a rapist. Ridiculous.

GARY SNOW

10. STREET HARASSMENT

Street harassment is also a very real thing and is something I really hate. I have had this happen when walking hand in hand with an ex-girlfriend of mine. A large group of young males asked if they could "have a pop" on my girlfriend as they so eloquently put it, and when I told them to "shut up" they actually tried to physically assault me while telling me to say sorry to them. And they would have succeeded with the assault if it wasn't for the security guards from the shop we were luckily walking into at the time.

No one should not feel like they are entitled to make sexually explicit comments about total strangers because they find them attractive. It's rude and inappropriate. As you can obviously tell from that story, this effects men too. Not just in the way I have described but I have also been wolf whistled and had random women slap my butt when in public.

Thing is, street harassment is never going to stop. Some people are just violent, abusive idiots who want to cause trouble and no amount of feminism will stop it. If this issue is to be tackled at all, it's a human rights issue not a gender specific feminist issue. It is intertwined with assault and it's generally the same type of people who do both of these things.

Also statistics show that men are the main victims of public violence. So the fact that feminists constantly complain about having things said to them and that makes the feel threatened. Men have to deal with actual, real threats and real violence on a far more regular basis than women.

But the thing that really bugs me is these videos of women wearing tight fitting clothes and purposefully walking through ghettos in order to get men to shout compliments at them. These incidents that occurred in isolated areas are nowhere near as bad as the real street harassment issues that face both men and women. Yet feminists act like it's the end of the world and they can't step out of their front door without being petrified of a man saying "hello" to them or telling them they're beautiful.

Surely assault is scarier than someone telling you they find you attractive. Surely getting mugged at knife point is worse than someone telling you are have nice eyes. Not for feminists apparently! Why do they think like this? Because these sexist feminists are scare mongering to get women to hate men by making them believe they live in a "rape culture".

We don't live in a rape culture, we just live in a world where some people, not some men but some people, are disgusting. It's a sad fact of life that feminism can't do anything about. Men can actually do more about this than women by correcting their friends if they show any signs of this sort of behavior. So why would you want a gender specific women's right movement to take control of this issue?

11. SEXUAL OBJECTIFICATION

In a non-sexual way, men objectify women and other men and women objectify men and other women. But this isn't mentioned until you bring sex into the equation. As sexual beings we sometimes objectify people in a sexual way because that's how the human brain works. Why this needs to keep being referenced by feminists when trying to generalize the male gender is completely beyond me.

This sexual objectification that feminists seem to love blaming men for, doesn't make any sense. If a man finds a woman sexually attractive and the woman wants him to find her sexually attractive then that's fine, he's just seeing her as someone he wants to have sex with. But if a man finds a women sexually attractive and the woman doesn't want him to find her sexually attractive then, according to feminists he's automatically objectifying her.

So if a man is walking down the road and he looks at a woman's breasts as she walks past because he finds them sexually attractive is this because he is seeing her as a sex object? Or is it just the fact that he liked the look of her breasts? The answer is, they're the same thing and there's nothing wrong with that.

Women also look at attractive men who they have never spoken to and think about them in a sexual way. This is the same thing as what men do to women and of course it's objectifying because you're looking at them as an object that you see in a sexual way without taking part of their personality into regards. We all do it!

This fits in with the very common feminist complaint that men tell them to smile. Guess what? I get told to smile all the time and I'm a man. In fact I got told to smile as a woman pulled up the corners of my mouth 3 days ago. I don't think many men would actually physically pull a woman's mouth about in order to get them to smile against their will. That sounds like a pretty weird thing to do right? Well no one batted an eyelid when it was done to me because I am a man so it was considered to be funny. While we're at it, I may as well tell you that the same girl proceeded to tickle me and no one cared about that either. If I had tickled her however I'm sure people would have thought I was some kind of weird creepy man.

That actually reminds me I was out having a drink with a friend about a month ago and a woman took a bit of a shine to me. I had never met her before and she was with a group of men and women who were listening to everything she said. She told me she was going to have sex with me and when I said "What if I don't want to?" she replied with "Well you don't have much of a choice". Everyone found this hilarious but what if I had said that to a random girl I had never met before? I would have probably been thrown out of the bar without a second thought.

If you disagree with any of this and still think that women have it bad, just remember, I have female friends that talk to me about guys they have been with. I know exactly how much women objectify men and judge them based on their height, build, penis size, bank balance, car, house, sexual skill, sexual stamina, how long they last in bed and much, much more besides.

Objectification affects us all and there is no way to stop it, so do me a favor feminists and stop talking about it like you're so hard done by.

12. MEN ARE NOT THE PROBLEM

I personally find it insulting when women say they see men as the cause of their problems. I'm a man and I don't go around wolf whistling women in the street or slapping their bums in nightclubs. I've had girls slap my bum, I've had girls in clubs sit on my lap and put their arms around me so that their boobs are pretty much in my face. As I said earlier, I have even had women tell me they are going to rape me. But that's not considered to be a problem, according to feminists that's what men do and men are the problem. What they should say is that people are the problem, not men.

This contributes to another huge problem that men face and that is constant sexism, I personally feel that I'm stereotyped and labelled as a sleaze bag by women on a daily basis just because I'm a man. I actually feel bad for walking behind a woman in the street, especially at night. But feminism doesn't care about how they are painting all men or how they are making us feel bad for being a man, just as long as they know I won't tell her she is pretty.

Man bashing feminists who think men are the problem and Beyoncé with her highly sexist "Who runs the world? Girls." statement seem to fail to realize the fact that the people who run the systems that keep us all living comfortably such as the government, the police, the fire service, the national grid are comprised of 90% men. If they got their wish, within 3 days of men leaving these positions and living up to the feminists expectations by being worthless pigs who are too useless to do anything, the mess that would ensue would take about 3 years to rectify.

In closing I will say this, the new wave of modern feminists do far more harm than good to our society and are especially damaging men's rights. We should all look out for each other. We should all fight for each other's rights. We should all educate those who are sexist towards men or women. We should fight for equality, not just rights of one sex or the other. We should be equalists.

Oh, and I'm undoubtedly going to get bad reviews by feminists who haven't even read the book so that less people buy it. So if you did enjoy the book please do consider leaving an honest review on Amazon so that I don't end up being another one they manage to silence for having an opinion of my own.

Thank you for reading.

GARY SNOW